Pebble®

Nature Basics

Soil Basics

by Carol K. Lindeen

Consulting Editor: Gail Saunders-Smith, PhD

Consultant: Sandra Mather, PhD
Professor Emerita of Geology and Astronomy
West Chester University, Pennsylvania

Capstone
Press®
Mankato, Minnesota

Pebble Books are published by Capstone Press,
151 Good Counsel Drive, P.O. Box 669, Mankato, Minnesota 56002.
www.capstonepress.com

1 2 3 4 5 6 12 11 10 09 08 07

Library of Congress Cataloging-in-Publication Data
Lindeen, Carol, 1976–
    Soil basics / by Carol K. Lindeen.
    p. cm.— (Pebble Books. Nature basics)
    Includes bibliographical references and index.
    ISBN-13: 978-1-4296-0003-3 (hardcover)
    ISBN-10: 1-4296-0003-9 (hardcover)
    1. Soils—Juvenile literature. 2. Soil ecology—Juvenile literature. I. Title.
II. Series.
S591.3.L56 2008
631.4—dc22   2006101954

Summary: Simple text and photographs present soil.

Note to Parents and Teachers

The Nature Basics set supports national science standards related
to earth and life science. This book describes and illustrates soil.
The images support early readers in understanding the text. The
repetition of words and phrases helps early readers learn new
words. This book also introduces early readers to subject-specific
vocabulary words, which are defined in the Glossary section. Early
readers may need assistance to read some words and to use the
Table of Contents, Glossary, Read More, Internet Sites, and Index
sections of the book.

Table of Contents

4

What Is Soil?

Soil is the top layer
of the earth.
Plants grow in soil.
Animals live in it
and on it.

6

Soil is made
of bits of rock.
Weather breaks
larger rocks into
these bits over time.

8

Rotting leaves
and animals
are also part of soil.

Types of Soil

Many types of soil are found on earth. Different rocks, plants, and animals make up each soil type.

Silt is soil that feels
like powder.
Wet silt turns into mud.
Dry silt blows away.

Soil made of clay
can clump together.
Wet clay is sticky
and heavy.
Dry clay is hard.

Soil made of
pebbles and sand
is loose and dry.

Living in Soil

Earthworms live in soil.
They eat rotting leaves.
Waste from earthworms
helps new plants grow.

Plants live in soil.
Plant roots soak up
food and water from soil.
What lives in
the soil near you?

Glossary

clay—very fine soil that is soft when wet and hard when dry

pebble—a small, round rock

powder—tiny grains of crushed rock

rot—to break down or decay; animals and plants rot after they die.

sand—tiny grains of rock

silt—particles of rock that are smaller than sand but larger than clay

waste—the material that is made and left behind by a living thing; animals eat food, use the minerals in the food, then get rid of the extra material as waste.

weather—the condition of the outdoors at a certain time and place; wind, rain, sleet, and snow can break rocks into smaller pieces.

Read More

Ballard, Carol. *How We Use Soil.* Raintree Perspectives. Chicago: Raintree, 2005.

Nelson, Robin. *Soil.* First Step Nonfiction. Minneapolis: Lerner, 2005.

Rosinsky, Natalie M. *Dirt: The Scoop on Soil.* Amazing Science. Minneapolis: Picture Window Books, 2003.

Internet Sites

FactHound offers a safe, fun way to find Internet sites related to this book. All of the sites on FactHound have been researched by our staff.

Here's how:

1. Visit *www.facthound.com*
2. Choose your grade level.
3. Type in this book ID **1429600039** for age-appropriate sites. You may also browse subjects by clicking on letters, or by clicking on pictures and words.
4. Click on the **Fetch It** button.

FactHound will fetch the best sites for you!

Index

Word Count: 140
Grade: 1
Early-Intervention Level: 18

Editorial Credits
Erika L. Shores, editor; Ted Williams, designer; Jo Miller, photo researcher

Photo Credits
BigStockPhoto.com/Adrian Jones, 10
Dreamstime/Bruce Macqueen, 4; Chee-onn Leong, 16; Sumeet Wadhwa, 8
Dwight R. Kuhn, 18
fotolia/Fedor Sidorov, 6
Getty Images Inc./Dorling Kindersley, 14
iStockphoto/Svetlana Prikhodko, 1
Shutterstock/Condor 36, 20; Mark Graves, 12; Sharon Kingston, cover (hand);
    Tina Rencelj, cover (plant)